A Color Guide to

YOGA

Howard Kent

CHARTWELL BOOKS INC.

ACKNOWLEDGEMENTS

All photographs are by Mark Gudgeon, except
those listed below:
Barnaby's Picture Library, pages 6, 8; Ray Green,
page 11; Picturepoint, pages 4, 5, 57, 58, 63, front
cover (center inset); Zefa, page 60.

Designed and produced by
 Intercontinental Book Productions,
Berkshire House, Queen Street,
Maidenhead, Berkshire, SLF INF

Printed in Hong Kong.

Contents

Why Practice Yoga?

Yoga started in the East, but is rapidly gaining favour in the West as well.

At first sight it seems strange that a philosophy and practice which are some thousands of years old and still thought of as Eastern and mystical, should have spread so widely across the world in the late twentieth-century. Why has this happened?

It would be easier to understand if yoga had arisen as a nine-day wonder – if, promoted by fashionable television and magazine publicity, it soared briefly and then dis-

appeared from view, as has been the fate of so many keep-fit crazes. On the contrary, yoga's popularity and influence are growing at an immense rate and show no signs of diminishing. Everything indicates that its future growth will be even more spectacular.

The answer to the apparent puzzle lies in the world around us. We are engulfed by the most pressurized society ever known; a mass society in which we sometimes feel we

Bad posture makes long hours even worse.

are entangled in a mighty machine which may well destroy us. We feel helpless, in the power of forces which we have no hope of controlling. As a result we feel there must be some way of living life at a more satisfactory level; some way in which the pressures are eased and, in seeking to find such a way, we hear of yoga. The amazing growth of yoga shows, quite simply, that it works.

Overcoming Stress

With up to thirty per cent of the entire adult population of the West suffering from definable hypertension, (my authority is the British Medical Journal), it is clear that stress problems of life today have reached massive proportions. Equally clearly, the yoga phenomenon demonstrates that it has an answer – I would say *the* answer – to this situation.

The aim of practicing yoga is to control the mind. Everything else is ancillary to this, for without mind control we are helpless. The health, happiness and advancement of human beings depends upon it. The stress under which we live is the measure of our failure to bring the mind into some semblance of order.

By mind control I mean the ability to marshal our thoughts, to direct them at will, so that we can study problems clearly and precisely and, from this, take decisions clearly and fearlessly. By maintaining this control over our lives we achieve a total transformation, for with that control comes *integration*. This is a feeling of one-ness,

which is man's natural state and from which we have become alienated.

This may seem to be a tall order, but it is in fact the nub of the problem and we should face it. The wonderful thing about yoga is that you can proceed very gently, step by step, so that the added peace, happiness and control happen virtually imperceptibly. You do not have to take grandiose decisions to change your life but, if you practice yoga *correctly*, the results will come. Whether you simply dip a toe in the water or plunge in headlong, you will feel the benefits and, because it is a natural process, you will find it ever more enjoyable, for there is nothing about yoga which is a strain or an irksome discipline.

Happiness and Health

Will yoga keep you healthy? Will it help you to slim? The answer to both these questions is Yes – if you realize these things are by-products of the main purpose of yoga: the calm, controlled mind. Bad health is all too often an outward and visible expression of an inward mental or emotional conflict. An overweight condition, equally, often comes from feelings of dissatisfaction and inadequacy. Deal with the central problems and its symptoms usually disappear.

Likewise our mental unhappiness is all too often created by the layers of conditioning we acquire through the years. We are what we think we are. We all can see this in others, but it is less easy to see it in ourselves.

When it comes to considering ourselves, the excuses – themselves self-created – spring all too readily to mind. We feel we are unique and misunderstood. We are all treated badly. Others do not realize just what we have to put up with!

While ensuring that we look facts square in the face, yoga can be used to create a whole new, more positive and optimistic outlook which changes the way we think.

I am not saying that if everyone practiced yoga there would be no unhappiness or ill-health – but I do think that our way of living would be transformed.

What is Yoga?

This yoga carving in fact comes from Java, but yoga has universal relevance, and its practice can benefit people from all corners of the globe.

Yoga is universal. Although the word itself comes from the ancient Sanscrit language and the practices we know as yoga principally developed in India, it is not simply a patent system but is man's path towards integration. It is a state in which we no longer find ourselves limited by our own individual pettiness.

What yoga affirms is that we *are* a part of all life and not isolated and lonely units. The famous Swiss psychologist, Carl Gustav Jung took much the same point of view when he wrote of the "collective unconscious".

Finding Your Self

We are all aware of dissatisfaction with ourselves. Much of our life is spent bemoaning to ourselves, "I wish I . . ." Who is this mysterious "I" who wishes to change "I"? Our lives, in fact, are to a great degree dominated by *internal* dialogues, conversations we hold with ourselves; trying to make up our minds about all sorts of decisions; prodding ourselves; excusing ourselves; trying to face up to problems; running away from problems. This all comes about because of what we call consciousness – layers within the brain which we know little about. Somewhere in these layers of consciousness lies the real 'I': the clear, steady, fearless, integrated personality which we are longing to realize. That person we call the Self. It is the essential unit of life within us and bears little or no relation to the outward and visible signs which are our body and our human personality.

We are aware of this central core when, contemplating a possible decision, we say, "I couldn't live with myself if I did that". Self is not only the conscience – it goes much deeper than that.

When we are run down, or tired, or bored, we become more and more aware of, and irritated by, our everyday self. When we are with someone in this state we declare that they " need to be taken out of themselves". In other words, that they be made less and less aware of their own small problems, by becoming absorbed in something more important. And that is the key word: absorbed. Here are two dictionary meanings of that important word: to swallow up the identity or individuality of; to engross fully. This is a word used to identify a state which we earnestly desire to achieve.

Yet our lives are spent at the very antithesis of this feeling: acutely aware of ourselves and our feelings and desires; ready to take offense, to be irritated or wounded; thrown back on ourselves, as we often say.

We can see from this that the truly desirable state of life is one in which we feel more and more absorbed – that is, less and less concerned with our own individual selves. Yoga is the path to such a feeling of absorption.

Practicing yoga does not mean that we retreat from the world and turn our back on the problems surrounding us. On the contrary, it gives us the strength to face them and the ability to deal with them sensibly.

We face them knowing we are greater than the problems, because fundamentally we are not alone but are part of, and supported by, the whole stream of life.

A New Approach to Life

More than two thousand years ago, one of the great sages of yoga, a man named Patanjali, declared: "Yoga is controlling the activities of the mind". His statement is as relevant today as ever. If our minds are in a mess, we are in a mess. If our minds are finding stability, we are finding stability. From stability springs a true feeling of peace, of one-ness.

A major problem we face in the current age, is that we have been conditioned to set our sights very low. We believe ourselves to be incapable of rising above our present state. We are conditioned to think that the trials of everyday living must prevent us from really enjoying life, except in all too brief spells and as a result we hardly even make an attempt. Small babies have an inbuilt urge to master the physical movement of their bodies. It must seem a daunting task to the baby to envisage walking, climbing, running, but the baby, not having been conditioned into accepting all sorts of limitations, has an inbuilt urge to make the body work and become the servant of the mind.

Later on, we find ourselves snowed under by mental images: genetic influences; parental influences; sensory impressions; memory, experience and suggestion. So many of these mental images are directed toward telling us what we cannot achieve, not what we can. So our minds become more cluttered and the idea of controlling them becomes more difficult. As a result we tend not even to try.

If we put into controlling our minds one-quarter of the effort which, as babies, we put into learning to walk, our lives would be changed beyond recognition. The techniques are not really difficult either, for they depend on achieving direct experience which can be gained relatively simply. Yoga shows us how.

Once, also, we realize this experience is universal we have come to understand another great aspect of life: it has total and absolute order, natural order, upon which we can rely. This order supports us when, experiencing it, we let ourselves into it.

Understanding Ourselves

The Buddha was one of the greatest yogis and is normally shown in the Lotus position.

The yoga symbol inset in the picture above is as precise as any contemporary scientific illustration and it is a symbol of the greatest significance.

The Forces Within Us

The Bible tells us: "In the beginning was the Word, and the Word was with God, and the Word was God." The concept of yoga is identical. All life springs from vibration and without it there can be no life, no planet, no universe. Vibration brings us sound, light . . . everything; it is based on polarity, a blending of two forces. In electricity we call these positive and negative. We all have electricity within us – our heart pumps electrically: messages pass between brain cells through electrical impulses. Our lives are even directly affected by the electricity in the atmosphere; one extreme example of this being when a thunderstorm builds up. We find it oppressive; sometimes it can give us headaches or it can even make us sick. The same positive and negative impulses within us also form part of our sexuality – using the word in its widest sense. We all have masculine and feminine tendencies, for these are not purely sexual in the way we superficially understand the word. That we end up as men and women is due to the balance of the chromosomes which make up part of the genetic chain, determining whether we are tall or short, naturally slim or plump, light or dark, and so on.

This dual functioning is a basic aspect of our lives. The balancing up of the forces within us is essential if we are to control our energy and, thereby, our mental balance. The natural relationship between man and woman is part of this process. Clearly, procreation has an important part to play in such relationships, but it is only one aspect of the whole situation. The fear of loneliness, which is such a potent factor in many people's lives, is a feeling of a lack of balance in life. Many of us proclaim that we are private people and that we find our own company very satisfying, yet this is never really sufficient. We need other people to supply us with some aspects of our life which we find lacking.

There is really no such thing as a solid human being. We are all built up of millions of cells. Each cell is separated from its neighbour and each is vibrating – it has a positive will to live and recreate itself. Comparatively few cells in the human body simply die out. This will to live is at the core of our existence.

How, you may ask, does all this affect us in our daily lives? It is important for us to know such things. We spend much of our lives enervating ourselves and promoting our own unhappiness and ill-health, by failing to understand the natural pattern of life and thereby blocking it. A failure to understand the flow of life will result in never-ending problems. Going with the flow of life will bring happiness and a deep sense of peace.

The Yoga Explanation

The simple yoga design shown on page 8 (inset), illustrates this pattern of life. It represents the two great polarizing factors – the up-pointing triangles representing the positive or masculine element; the down-painting triangles, the negative or feminine element; the dot in between represents vibration. To a degree we can associate the negative impulse with rationality and the positive with creativity. This can be seen within the human brain.

Yoga knowledge has always postulated that the left-hand side of the body is the rational or electrically negative side, while the right hand is the creative or electrically positive one. This has seemed a far-fetched conclusion to Western scientists for many years, until recent research on the human brain has revealed some significant factors. It is now known that the left lobes of the brain house the rational faculties, such as speech, while the right lobes contain the creative faculties, including movement. Sir John Eccles, who has won the Nobel Prize for his research on the human brain, states categorically that he finds creative people, such as artists, use the right lobes of the brain to a far greater degree than others. He also comments that he has discovered this division of function of the lobes to be the case in 98 per cent of the brains he has examined. This, of course, appears to tally with the yoga concept.

It cannot be too strongly stressed that our whole lives are a search for balance and stillness. It is significant that parents nearly always wish that their children will be happier, more balanced people than they have been themselves. This is not merely an accident, it is because the whole of life is moving towards this balance, which is described by the Christian religion as "the peace which passeth all understanding".

We should not be deluded by the fact that our society tends to oppose these essential aspects of man's development. We have established restlessness in place of peace, noise in place of silence and we are suffering as a result. This state has in fact been brought about by a society based upon the manufacture of objects rather than one which understands the essential non-material foundation of human peace and happiness.

To rely solely upon external objects for our satisfaction is to take a path which can only end in emptiness and disillusion. No true feeling of satisfaction can ever be achieved this way.

If we begin to understand our own lives in these terms, we have taken the first step towards obtaining that balance and peace, for the understanding opens up the doorway to a happier, more fulfilled life. At such a time we find that satisfaction is something which wells deep within us and does not rely on external stimulation.

Understanding our Energy

Although we know a great deal about our bodies, we know far less about our minds. But we know that the two are totally interlinked – the mind dictates many of the activities of the body and the state of the body can affect the working of the mind. How, then, can we apply controls which will benefit both body and mind?

Controlling Body Energy

A standard medical text book will describe how oxygen is absorbed through the lungs into the blood stream and how complicated processes take place within us to absorb the nutrients from food. This, however, constitutes only a small part of the process which we know as body energy. The whole flow of energy, which includes the electromagnetic force through the body, is described in yoga as *Prana*, or *Life Force*. Although not yet generally accepted in medical circles, the force of Prana is being taken very seriously by more and more research workers. Freed and able to flow through the body, it can stimulate both body and mind; blocked and distorted, it can sap and deplete our activities.

Breathing

The center of the energy flow is respiration, for which the movement of the diaphragm is of the greatest importance. The diaphragm is the tough sheet of muscle which stretches under the rib cage and which *should* move up and down as we breathe. Unfortunately present day shallow breathing patterns often inhibit the use of this vital muscle. In our modern life style, many people spend most of the day sitting at desks, hunched up over factory benches, or working at home chores. These positions inhibit proper chest and diaphragm movement. The polluted atmosphere we breathe also affects the lungs and our natural reaction is to breathe less deeply, to keep out as much of the poison as possible.

If we want confirmation of the effect of breathing patterns on vital energy, we have only to study certain groups of people. Pictures of prisoners of war and unemployed from depressed areas often show men with drooping shoulders squeezing the lungs, so that only limited breathing takes place. Their breathing pattern expresses their dejection and because it echoes this state it also makes it worse. Old people, too, often fall into this fatal trap. Many stoop and reduce their whole breathing efficiency which, in turn, further depletes their energy, so they droop even more.

A happy man, even if he is unaware of breathing techniques, naturally pulls back his shoulders and breathes with greater depth and rhythm. It is quite easy for you to become aware of your own breathing patterns and to notice how they will follow your state of mind.

If you are feeling peaceful and relaxed, your breathing will be relaxed and instinctively controlled. You will especially notice that your exhalation is quite slow and unhurried. If you are tense your breath pattern speeds up; it becomes irregular and nearer a gasp than a calm breath. The exhalation is particularly affected and becomes a short, violent pushing out of stale air.

In both cases the breathing pattern echoes the state of mind. From this realization, it is not difficult to understand that conversely by *controlling* the breath you can have a direct effect upon the state of the mind. For the way the mind functions is largely determined by the way in which the supply of oxygen and Life Force is directed.

Most of us have experienced that depressing state when we awake in the early hours of the morning and feel that life is one long disaster area. If we eventually drop off to sleep and wake some hours later, in the light of the morning things don't look nearly so bad. The problems which looked insoluble are, in fact, not very serious at all. This happens because of the shallow way in which we breathe during the night and because, as a result of depleting body energy, our body temperature drops. This activates the brain in such a way as to make our problems seem overwhelming. Even then, our consciousness tells us that this is a one-sided picture, but we are unable to escape from the pattern which we have built up by the depletion of our energy sources.

Better Breathing Techniques

To begin to gain control of our energy flow and thereby of our mind activity, we must have direct experience of control. This is achieved both by helping the diaphragm to function and to increase its elasticity, and by opening the rib cage, so that the lungs have a proper chance of expansion.

As a start in this direction, use a room which is warm and free from draughts. If there is no carpet, use a mat or rug to lie on. Wear simple clothes which do not constrict you. Lie down on the mat or carpet, allowing your back to lie flat on the floor. This is best achieved by laying your trunk on the ground first, with knees bent and then sliding your legs down on the floor, until you are lying flat. The legs should be at least a foot apart and, because the ankles are slack, the toes will splay outwards. Your arms should be well away from your sides, with the palms upwards and no tension in the wrists. Your head must be in a straight line with your body, with the neck gently stretched. Once correctly in this position you are lying in the most relaxed way possible.

Now listen to your breath and become totally aware of it. You will feel the cool touch of the air as it reaches your nostrils when you breathe in, and the warm flow of air as you breathe out. Be aware of this, feel that the length of the flow is under your control and totally rhythmical. Make sure that the exhalation takes longer than the inhalation.

After you have lain in this manner for a short time, become aware of the movement of your body. You will find that as you

This young Yorkshire miner's posture can only serve to make his exhaustion worse.

breathe in, your abdomen is gently rising and as you breathe out it is falling, equally gently. This is the natural movement as your diaphragm gently moves with your breath. Maintain the awareness of the sound of your breath, the feeling of the breath and the movement of the body. Feel that it is totally controlled by your mind. In this way you are beginning to set up a pattern which will achieve instant recognition in the brain.

After you have practiced for a few days you will find it coming more and more easily. Never practice for less than ten minutes: set the time aside and realize that it is more important to you than so many of the rushed activities which you fit in every day.

Releasing Body Energy

Once you feel truly happy and relaxed with this type of breathing, direct your consciousness to the rib cage and feel that every time you breathe in, the ribs expand. Feel especially the lower ribs stretching up and out, for from this movement will stem greater elasticity in the diaphragm. Also, feel that the movement is totally under control and that the exhalation is long and peaceful.

To monitor your breath, become aware that it passes through the nostrils to the throat and that by a slight constriction in the throat you can control the exhalation. To find this for yourself, first of all breathe in and out with the mouth open and listen to the sound at the back of your throat. When you have observed and understood this sound, close your mouth, breathe through the nostrils and still feel the control. This should be especially pronounced when you breathe out and by using the throat as a control valve, you will slow the exhalation and hear the sound of the air escaping at the back of your throat. Persist until you achieve this naturally and feel it combining with the gentle rhythm of the breath and the movement of the body. Now you have reached the stage when you can experience an internal stillness from which the body energy can flow unblocked, and from the flow of body energy the mind can work toward peaceful control.

Controlling Tension

While the brain is the great nerve center of the body, there are other areas which play vital and specific roles in our lives. Two of these are of special importance. The first is what we call the Solar Plexus area: a point at which the activity of the nerves is so great that it is often called the Second Brain. This is the sensitive area of stress and tension in the body. We all know how we tense up here whenever we are worried or on edge. We complain of "butterflies in the stomach". Functioning properly, this area is of immense importance to our health and vitality; if tension sets in the functioning becomes distorted and health problems quickly arise.

The second vital area is the Cardiac Plexus or Heart Center. This is the spot at which we feel our emotions of love and affection. It is not the heart itself, but the major nerve center which is responsible for the body functions in this area and therefore has a direct affect on the pumping of the heart.

In yoga these centers are called *chakras* or wheels, for they are points at which a high, unimpeded energy flow must be maintained. Both our tensions and our resulting poor breathing deplete this energy flow and the result is harmful – often disastrous.

Starting from the simple but profound breathing technique which has been described, linking this with the movement of the yoga postures, we can begin to bring our tension under control, build up the body energy control and calm the mind. This is the road to peace and health.

We must realize, however, that essential though a correct appreciation of breathing may be, it can only provide a foundation upon which we have to build. In this respect yoga helps us to understand that the path of life can be considered as rather like building a house.

We are all keen to rush ahead and put up the structures of our own imagining, without necesarily ensuring that the correct foundations have first been laid. But of course, just as a house built without the right structural foundations will fall, so our lives will be unsettled and unhappy if we omit the basis of the correct flow of energy based on the breath. What structure we decide to erect on top of that, however, will still depend on a whole number of factors. Breathing is very important to yoga, therefore, and it allows us to postulate the twin pillars of energy flow and the control of the mind.

It is for this reason that down through the ages yoga sages have seen that the breath can symbolize the whole of life, both physical and mental. Phsyiologically, each in-breath brings air containing oxygen into the body and stimulates our energy. It is thus an act of tension and the entire neuro-muscular system is put on alert to tense as we breathe in. Psychologically, the in-breath can be seen as an expression of the will to live, and someone who is afraid of life will have difficulty in breathing in.

Likewise, the out-breath is physically a relaxation and the muscles will relax with the breath. Psychologically, it is letting go; accepting rather than struggling. Once we understand and accept these natural aspects the breath can give us wonderful help in our everyday lives.

The yoga exercises are designed to stimulate the *chakras,* or energy centers, seen as wheels within us.

Understanding our Bodies

Yoga postures are called *asanas* – a Sanscrit word meaning 'holding a seat'. They have all developed from a series of body movements devised specifically to control the mind. Because they are natural positions, using the whole of the body correctly while they are helping us to achieve mind control, they also perform invaluable physiological functions. Thus, while yoga movements are performed slowly and with great concentration because of the mind control basis, this method of performance tones the neuro-muscular system; at the same time it also encourages the flow of blood through the nerves, strengthens the joints and encourages the balanced activity of the glands and organs.

It is only in recent years that we have come to understand the amazing subtlety of body function and the fact that everything in our life is based upon a variety of rhythmical patterns. We are dominated by the force patterns which are set up by the interplay of sun, moon and planets – scientists call this the Circadian Pattern, a cycle of approximately twenty-four hours. Interfering with this pattern through modern air travel brings the state we know as jet lag. Shift workers, especially those with varying shifts, fall victim to similar symptoms.

The slow, calm, controlled nature of movements in yoga stimulates the correct functioning of the body's intricate rhythm pattern. In the same way that the malfunctioning of one small part can bring a huge machine to a halt, so a similar minor physiological imbalance can seize up the whole working of our body.

It cannot be too strongly stressed that everything in yoga is achieved by relaxation. The more we strain to achieve effect, the more distorted the effect will be.

Thus it is important to move into the *asanas* with awareness, not inhibiting oneself with stressful thoughts which will result in all sorts of irrelevant muscles being tensed and strained in a mistaken endeavor to obtain a right result.

Preparing for Yoga Exercises

To practice the postures shown on the following pages, you need to approach every session in a calm, relaxed way. Choose the amount of time you are giving to your session, and clear the mind of all worries. It is important first of all to lie down for a few minutes, breathing slowly and gently and becoming aware of the rise and fall of the abdomen. Allow the body to relax and be still.

Then, before you start the exercises stretch the body gently but thoroughly.

Always choose a room which is comfortable and without draughts, have something suitable, such as a rug or carpet, to exercise on and wear sensible clothing that is neither too floppy nor too tight. If you are in the privacy of your own home you need not wear any clothing at all.

Never hurry a posture; always keep your mind concentrated on it, and always coordinate wholly with the breath. Let your own awareness tell you what to do and how long to spend on it. If you truly "tune in" to your body it will be quite explicit in its instructions.

Never try to practice anything you do not understand; you can do more harm than good. Unless you have natural suppleness, ensure that postures such as the Lotus or Headstand are taught you by qualified instructors.

Finish, also, on a short relaxation; do not destroy the mood of peace and rhythm you have created.

Remember that however busy you believe yourself to be, a good portion of every day is wasted by muddled thinking and indecision. A session of yoga helps to eliminate this waste.

A leotard and warm tights are suitable clothes for yoga exercises, allowing free movement but not getting in your way.

Lotus

You should only attempt the Lotus position if you have been taught how to do it by a qualified instructor. Like all the postures, you should never have to strain yourself. If you cannot achieve the full Lotus in comfort, try a half Lotus, putting one foot on the ground close to the body and the other on, or just in front of, the opposite thigh.

Fig 1

Fig 2

Fig 3

Fig 4

Fig 1

Palm Tree

Before you begin any session of yoga postures spend a few minutes stretching, to put your body into a suitable condition for the movements you are about to perform. Do the stretches slowly, combine them with the breath and be very aware of what you are doing.

Fig 1: Stand with feet together and hands by your sides, backs of the hands facing the front. Breathe out, then slowly breathe in, bringing the arms up in front of you and at the same time rising up on your toes. Stretch the arms right above the head. Maintain your balance, stretching all the time. Breathing slowly out, bring down the arms, this time stretching them out to the sides. Do not come off your toes – and then slowly – until your palms have touched your thighs.

Fig 2: Link fingers and raise arms above the head, stretching hard and breathing in.

Fig 3: Breathe out, still stretching, and then, breathing in again, bend backwards, pulling the arms back also.

Fig 4: Breathing out, bend forward, keeping the back straight and still stretching the arms.

Figs 5 and 6: Come up again, breathing in and bend first to the right and then to the left. Finally, bring the arms down to the side again, breathing out.

Fig 6

Salute to the Sun

Salute to the Sun (Surya Namaskar) is, obviously, an oblation to our dependance on the sun's rays. A brilliantly devised sequence, it stretches and tones the whole body. Ideally, it should be performed with total concentration on the breath and the sun.

Fig 1: Stand upright and well-balanced. Breathing out, bring the hands to the chest in a prayer position.

Fig 2: Breathing in, swing the arms over the head, thrusting out the hips to counter-poise the body.

Fig 3: Breathing out, sweep the arms down and place the hands each side of the feet. If you can not reach the ground with the hands, make sure they are aligned with the feet and not in front of them. Let the head hang.

Fig 4: Keeping the hands and right foot fixed, breathe in, taking the left leg back, with the knee touching the ground. Look ahead.

Fig 5: Holding the breath, bring the right leg back and hold the body level, like a plank. Look ahead.

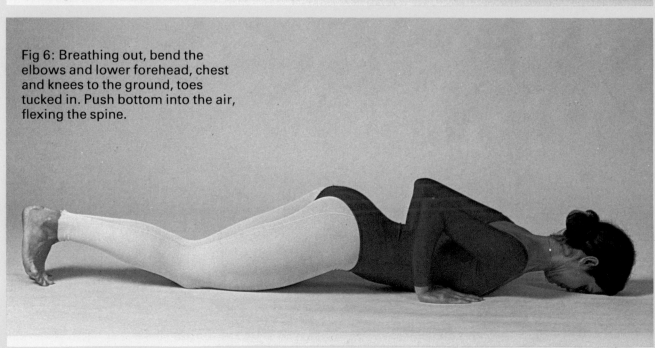

Fig 6: Breathing out, bend the elbows and lower forehead, chest and knees to the ground, toes tucked in. Push bottom into the air, flexing the spine.

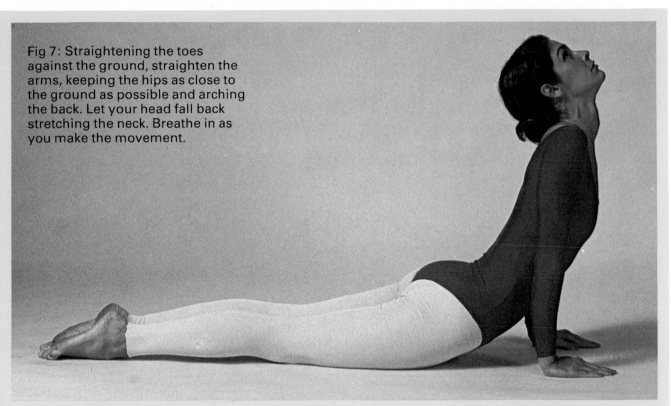

Fig 7: Straightening the toes against the ground, straighten the arms, keeping the hips as close to the ground as possible and arching the back. Let your head fall back stretching the neck. Breathe in as you make the movement.

Fig 8: Tucking the toes in, and breathing out, straighten the legs, so you are resting on feet and hands with the back as high as possible in the air. Let the head dangle. Press the heels against the ground.

23

Fig 9: Breathing in, straighten the body and bring the right leg up to between the hands. Look ahead.

Fig 10: Breathing out, bring up the left leg and straighten both legs, keeping the hands on the ground.

NOTE: The hands do not move at all during the sequence. If you cannot place your hands flat on the floor while your legs are unbent, make sure that the tips of the fingers touch the floor firmly and that the palms come flat down as the movements bend the legs.

Fig 11: Straighten up, breathing in and swinging the arms above your head, bending backwards.

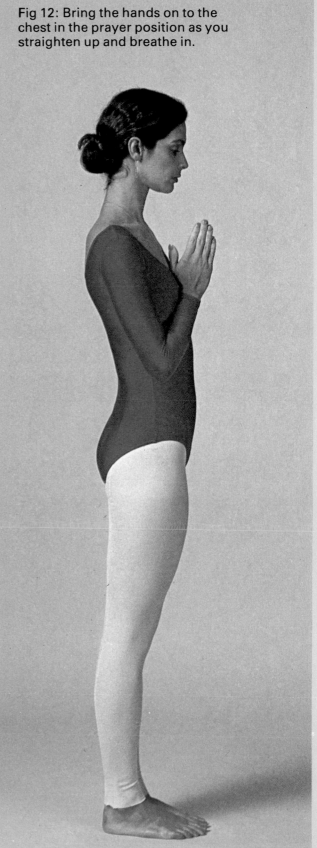

Fig 12: Bring the hands on to the chest in the prayer position as you straighten up and breathe in.

Posterior Stretch

This exercise stretches the neck, spine, back muscles, thigh and calf muscles and puts a valuable compression on the visceral area. It requires relaxation and breath control.

Fig 1: Sit on the ground with the feet together in front of you, toes pulled up. Make sure you are sitting on the bones of the bottom and hold your back erect. Breathe out.

Fig 2: Breathing in, stretch the arms into the air above your head, palms pointing forwards.

Fig 3: Breathing slowly out, stretch yourself forward, keeping the chin jutting out and the back erect. As you feel the back is being stretched to its maximum, allow it to bend and the head to drop on or close to the calves. Try to clasp the feet, or bring the hands together around the feet, keeping the legs straight. If you cannot get down to the full position, clasp the outsides of your feet, ankles or thighs and each time you breathe out, bend the elbows downwards, to stretch you further down. Be totally aware of the breath and work with it. Finally, come up again breathing in.

Cobra

The counterbalancing position to the Posterior Stretch, this is one of the great classical postures of yoga. Again, be careful to work with the breath.

Fig 1: Lie on your tummy, with feet together, hands by the sides, palms down and forehead against the floor. Breathe slowly out.

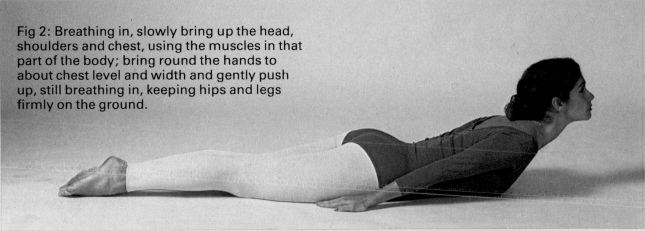

Fig 2: Breathing in, slowly bring up the head, shoulders and chest, using the muscles in that part of the body; bring round the hands to about chest level and width and gently push up, still breathing in, keeping hips and legs firmly on the ground.

Fig 3: Straighten the arms, to provide the strongest support for your trunk and bring the head back to stretch the neck. Breathe gently in the position and feel the spine relax with every out-breath. When you come down, breathe out as you do so and return to the floor very slowly, completing every movement. Then relax totally.

Side Bend

The most famous of the yoga side bends is known as the Triangle. It is a remarkable exercise, not merely for achieving suppleness, but also for securing real body balance.

Fig 1

Fig 2

Fig 1: Stand with legs reasonably well apart. Point the right foot directly away from the body, the left foot just pointing towards the right foot, with the right heel in line with the left instep. Square up the trunk to the legs.

Fig 2: Breathe in and stretch out the arms, tightening the leg muscles. Then, retaining the breath, push the hips over to the left.

Fig 3: Breathing out, begin to bend to the right, letting the right hand slide down the outside of the right leg. At the same time, look at the left hand, turning the palm to face the front and bringing it up horizontal. When you have finished breathing out, the right hand should be holding the right foot or ankle, with the head over the foot. Look at the hand in the air the whole time. Come slowly up breathing in. Repeat on the other side.

Twist

Twisting the spine provides some of the greatest strengthening for this vital part of the body, also helping the nervous system. Make sure the body is well-balanced.

Fig 1: Sit on the ground with the legs in front of you and the back erect. Pull the toes towards you.

Fig 2: Breathing in, bend the left leg, raising it over the right leg, and place the foot on the ground by the right knee joint.

Fig 3: Breathing out, place the left hand (palm on the ground) behind you parallel with the spine, and bring the right hand up so that the arm presses the left knee into the chest and you grasp the left ankle. Turn the shoulders to the left and look over the left shoulder. Breathe gently in position. Repeat on the other side.

Shoulder Stand

Performed in a relaxed fashion, the Shoulder Stand promotes relaxation, improves circulation, aids the heart, regularizes the thyroid gland and helps calm the mind. Balance will make it possible to hold the position for several minutes at a time, but do not take account of the passing of time, work to the impulse within you.

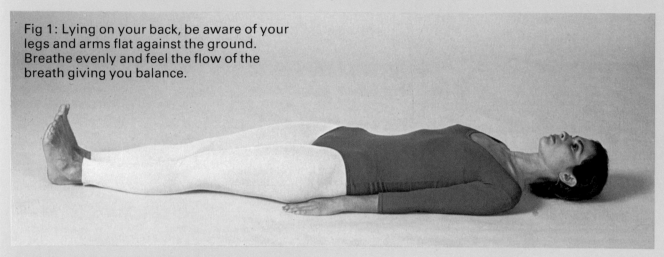

Fig 1: Lying on your back, be aware of your legs and arms flat against the ground. Breathe evenly and feel the flow of the breath giving you balance.

Fig 2: Breathing in, swing the legs over the head and as the bottom comes off the ground press down with your elbows, bringing the trunk into the air.

Fig 3: Make sure the trunk is almost vertical (keeping neck and shoulders relaxed) and that the chin is firmly pressing into the jugular notch at the top of the chest. Point the toes and then pull the heels away, to give the legs maximum stretch. Then let the ankles be relaxed, so the feet fall parallel with the ground. Breathe evenly. When coming down, *first* bring the arms down on the ground, so the palms can support the weight of the legs, then swing the legs back over the head and slowly back to the ground, maintaining total control.

Fish

The Shoulder Stand stretched the cervical vertebrae in the neck. The Fish compacts them. It is used, therefore, as the perfect counter exercise to this position.

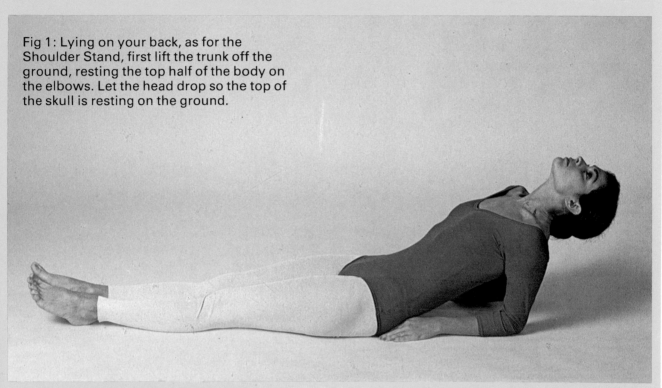

Fig 1: Lying on your back, as for the Shoulder Stand, first lift the trunk off the ground, resting the top half of the body on the elbows. Let the head drop so the top of the skull is resting on the ground.

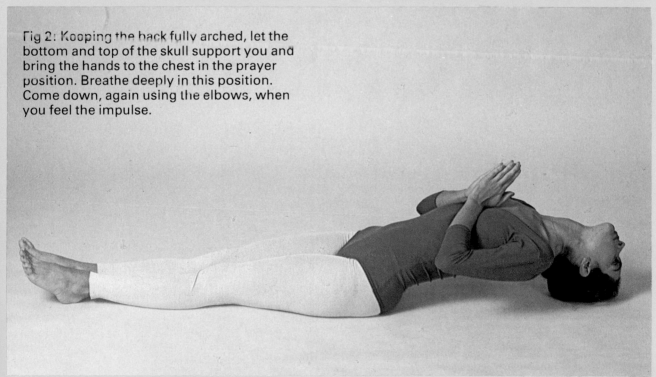

Fig 2: Keeping the back fully arched, let the bottom and top of the skull support you and bring the hands to the chest in the prayer position. Breathe deeply in this position. Come down, again using the elbows, when you feel the impulse.

Cat

Flexibility of the spine is of the greatest importance and this is achieved particularly efficiently in the Cat posture. Performed regularly and correctly this posture will promote both suppleness and a toning of the nervous system.

Fig 1: Get down on all fours, with the hands resting firmly on the palms, about shoulder width apart. Breathe out.

Fig 2: Breathing in, lift the head and stretch the back downwards, keeping the arms and legs still. Keep moving until the breath stops.

Fig 3: Breathing out, drop the head and bend the back into the air, again co-ordinating the movement with the breath. Continue this several times.

Fig 4: Finally, after breathing out, breathe in again letting the hips come forward as close as they can to the ground, head back. This is a similar position to the Cobra except that the arms will be straighter. Follow this by breathing out, straightening the legs and bringing up the back (the Dog pose) as you did in the Salute to the Sun (p.20).
Finally, get back on all fours, sink on to your heels, let the forehead touch the floor and place the hands by the sides, palms up. Relax in this position, breathing gently.

Camel

The Camel is an important back stretch, which is also extremely beneficial for thigh and abdominal areas. Another benefit is learning to overcome the fear of groping backwards to grasp the ankles while arching the hips forward. This, achieved in balance, helps create confidence. It is important to thrust the hips forward while breathing in, and to hold the position in a relaxed manner while breathing out. Constant practice of this exercise will aid greatly the suppleness of the muscles on the front of the thighs.

The Bridge has similar virtues and is performed in a reclining position.

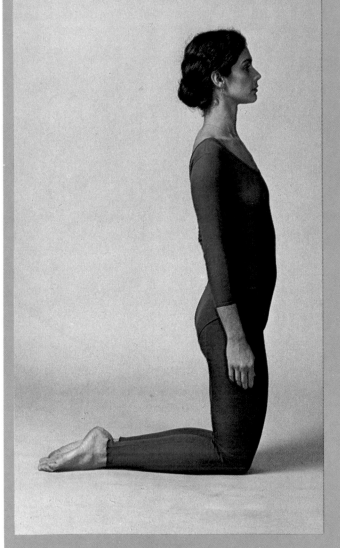

Fig 1: Sit erect on your heels, insteps flat against the ground, arms hanging by the side, head well balanced. Breathe evenly.

Fig 2: Breathing in, arch the spine backwards, allowing the head to drop back and pushing out the hips. At the same time, let the arms fall back to grasp the ankles. When both ankles are firmly grasped, use the breath to increase the arch. Hold the position every time you breathe in and push the hips a little further forward as you breathe out. If you have difficulty at first in grasping the ankles, let one hand move back at a time.

Bridge

Fig 1: Lie on your back, breathing evenly, and bend the knees, bringing the feet close into the bottom.

Fig 2: As you breathe in, arch the back into the air and bring the left hand under the left hip, leaving the other hand still on the ground. Push up with the hand as the breath takes the trunk up.

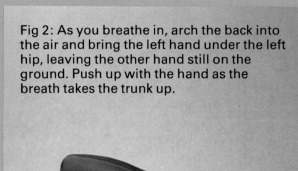

Fig 3: Bring up the right hand into a similar position to the left. Continue to raise the trunk on each out-breath. Hold until the impulse tells you to come down, removing one hand at a time.

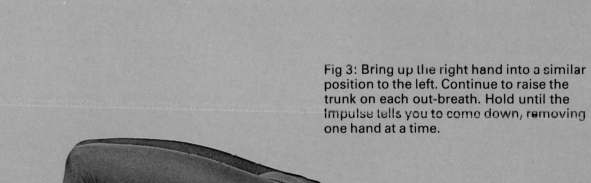

Locust

Two excellent dynamic postures of yoga are the Locust and the Bow. Each of these depends upon co-ordination of mental instruction, breath and muscular tension. They should be built up naturally, based on ever-increasing relaxation of mind.

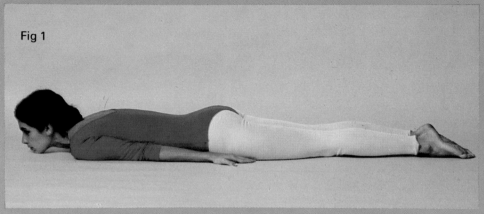

Fig 1

Fig 1: Lie on your tummy, arms by the side, palms down, chin against the floor. Make fists of your hands with the thumbs tucked in, and place them in the groin area.

Fig 2

Fig 2: Breathing evenly, raise up one leg on an in-breath, not allowing either the leg to bend at the knee joint or the hips to move off the ground. Hold, breathing gently, and then slowly lower back to the ground. Repeat with the other leg.

Fig 3

Fig 3: Increase the strength of the breath and feel the energy it gives you. On an in-breath swing both legs and hips off the ground, pressing hard down with the fists. Hold the position a few seconds on the held breath and then slowly come down again, breathing out.

Bow

Fig 1: First lie on your tummy in the same position as for the Locust. Then bend one leg and grasp the foot or ankle. Next bend the other leg and hold it similarly.

Fig 2: Again paying full attention to the breath, pull on the feet and raise the chest simultaneously, seeking to lift the thighs off the ground. Keep the head well up. If you are comfortable, rock to and fro on your tummy, like a rocking horse. Lower the legs slowly on an out-breath.

Boat

The Boat and the Canoe both demand co-ordination and intelligent muscle control. Their value to the visceral area is tremendous and they require great concentration.

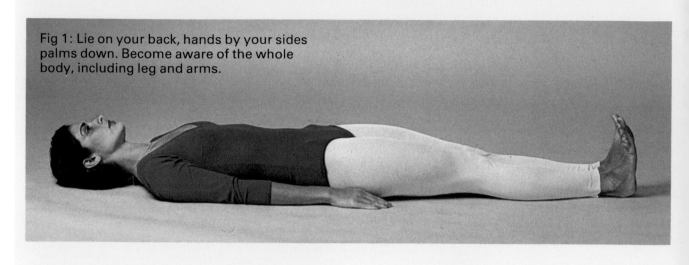

Fig 1: Lie on your back, hands by your sides palms down. Become aware of the whole body, including leg and arms.

Fig 2: On an in-breath raise the legs straight into the air. Then raise the arms and trunk, so that the arms, parallel with the ground, come each side of the raised legs. Hold for a short time, retaining the breath and then come down in this order: first, unwind the back on to the ground, vertebra by vertebra; next, slowly bring down the arms; finally, gently lower the legs and then relax completely.

Canoe

Fig 1: Lie on your tummy, with your chin on the floor, arms by your sides palms down.

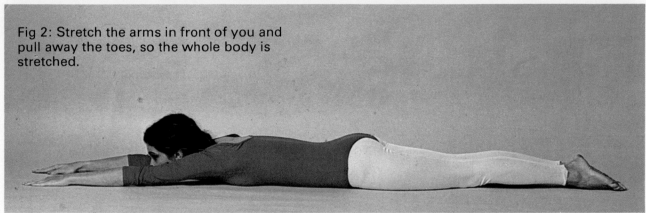

Fig 2: Stretch the arms in front of you and pull away the toes, so the whole body is stretched.

Fig 3: On an in-breath, raise both arms and legs in the air, so you are resting on your tummy. Keep the stretch and make sure the head is raised. Hold for a few seconds and come slowly down on the impulse.

Balancing

Physical balancing is of the utmost importance to us and yoga balancing poses can
make an immense difference to our whole
body awareness. The secret lies in concentration. Always fix your gaze on an immov-
able object at about eye level and take your
consciousness into the throat, for this is the
body's centre of steadiness.

For all balancing positions, stand with feet
together and back erect. Arms by the side and
head well balanced. Apart from maintaining the
erect spine, the body is to be kept relaxed –
especially note and eliminate any tension in
shoulders and neck.

Tree

Bring one foot into the groin, lifting it into position
with the hands. Bring the knee out as widely as
you can. Then carefully raise the arms over the
head, palms touching, and stretch up, so that the
arms touch the ears. Maintain this postion,
breathing gently. Come down slowly, lifting the
bent leg down with the hands. Repeat on the
other side. If you cannot get the foot into the
groin, place it against the opposite knee to start
with.

Dancer

Stretch the right arm in front of you; bend the left leg with the foot upwards and clasp the foot with the left hand, pulling the leg up to stretch the thigh, arching the back. Repeat, on the other side.

Eagle

This is an exceptionally good posture for rheumatic joints. Lift one leg and bend it around the other so that the toes eventually rest against the calf of the straight leg. Then twist one arm around the other, linking the hands. Finally bend the knee of the straight leg. Repeat, changing the leg and arms.

Rabbit

This is a sequence of breathing postures which help to use each breathing area of the lungs. The various postures control the muscles so that only the required sections of the chest can be relaxed to admit the air into the lungs.

Fig 1

Fig 1: Sit on your heels, with elbows and palms on the ground in front of you and look ahead of you. Your tummy will be pressing against your thighs. As you breathe out, feel the tummy move away from the thighs. Then breathe in, feeling the tummy expand like a balloon as the diaphragm pushes down. The chest does not move. Repeat slowly several times.

Fig 2

Fig 2: Sit up on the heels, with the palms on the ground by the knees, shoulder width apart. Breathe out, pulling in the tummy muscles. Then breathe in, letting the tummy be gently held and feeling the chest expanding. Repeat slowly several times.

Fig 3: Starting in the same position as in Fig 2, breathe out while lowering the head, finishing with the crown of the head on the ground a little ahead of the palms.

Fig 4: Now breathe in while pushing forward on the crown of the head, opening the back of the neck. This directs the air into the top portion of the lungs. Keeping the crown of the head on the ground, move back, removing the stretch from the neck and breathing out. Repeat slowly several times and then come up breathing in.

Hill Breath

Yoga has a variety of breathing exercises, many of which (Pranayama) are for deep meditation purposes. The exercises on this and the following three pages are more physiological in their benefits.

Those with lung trouble should be

Fig 1: Stand with the legs together, arms by the side and breathe out slowly and deeply, contracting the tummy muscles as the chest falls. Then start breathing in, raising the arms by the side, but keeping them stretched so the hands are a little behind the shoulders. Co-ordinate the breath with the movement, at first allowing the abdomen to expand (*not* pushing it out) and then the chest to expand.

Fig 2

Fig 2: Stretching all the time, bring the arms up so that eventually the thumbs touch or link and the arms are just behind the ears. The thumbs should touch as the last breath comes in the body. Muscles of abdomen and chest will now be firmly held. Retain the breath for some seconds and then slowly bring down the arms, still stretching and co-ordinating the out-breath with the arm movement. Repeat several times.

Squeeze Breath

careful when trying breathing exercises and not push the lungs beyond capacity. On the other hand, gently carried out with aware-ness these exercises can be of great benefit. If in doubt consult either your doctor or a qualified yoga instructor.

Fig 1: This is an excellent exercise for clearing the passages of the lungs and eliminating mucous blockages. Begin as for the Hill Posture but bend the arms and bring the fingertips to the shoulders, with the in-breath.

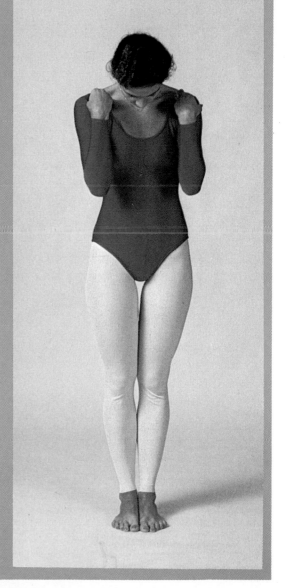

Fig 2: Retaining the breath, bring down the head and shoulders and bring in the elbows, reducing the lung capacity and squeezing the air in the lungs. Hold a few seconds and then bring the hands down again breathing out. Repeat once or twice.

Hanuman Postures

These are known as the Hanuman Postures. Hanuman was a monkey king who came to the aid of Prince Rama when his wife was abducted by a demon in the forest, in a classical Indian story. These exercises are very valuable for expanding the chest, toning the chest muscles and making full use of the lungs while stretching the body.

Fig 1: Standing with feet together, take a stride forward and lunge, bending the knee so that calf and thigh are at right angles. Stretch out the arms in front of you, breathing out.

Fig 2

Fig 2: Breathing strongly in, swing the arms back over the head, arching the back. Hold a few seconds and then bring the arms slowly back, breathing out. Repeat once or twice, with each leg.

Fig 3: Lunge similarly to the first exercise, but this time make fists of the hands, extend the elbows and hold the arms as though holding a spring across the chest, breathing out.

Fig 4: Breathing in, pull out the fists, tensing the muscles, squeezing the shoulder blades towards one another, opening the chest laterally. Breathe out, bringing the arms back. Repeat once or twice with each leg.

Fig 3

Fig 4

Posture Clasp

The Posture Clasp and the Lion both take tension out of the shoulders and face, and the Lion, despite its peculiarity, tones all face muscles and benefits the throat.

Fig 1

Fig 1: Sit on your heels with hands on your thighs. Bring the right arm behind the head and place it on the back. Bend the left arm so the hand comes up the back and let the two hands grasp. Breathe in and then, breathing out, bend slowly down until your forehead touches your knees. Come slowly up breathing in.

Fig 2 shows a back view of the posture. Repeat on the other side (Fig 3). If you cannot link the hands a handkerchief may be used. You will find that the arms will link more easily when the arm behind the head is the arm you normally use for writing.

Fig 2

Fig 3

Lion

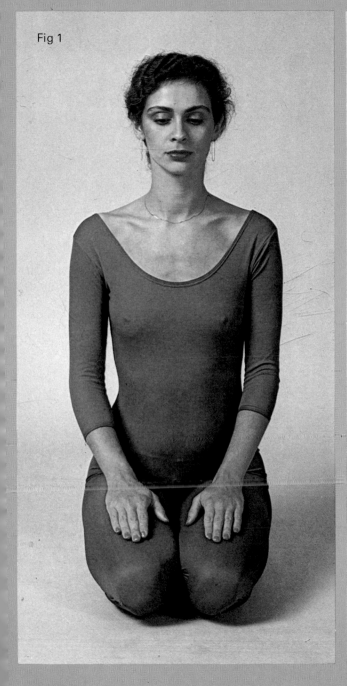

Fig 1

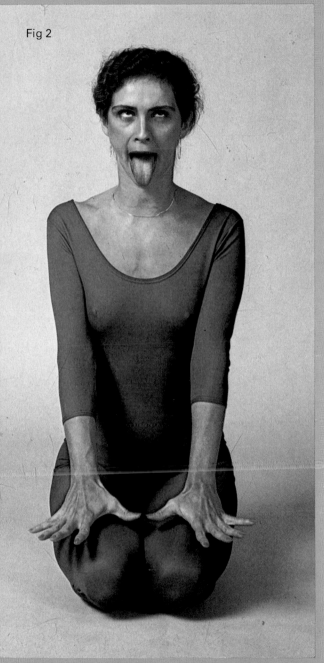

Fig 2

Fig 1: Sit on your heels, back erect, otherwise relaxed, with hands on the thighs. Breathe out.

Fig 2: Breathe in sharply and then breathe out quickly through the mouth, extending the tongue so the tip is against the chin, tensing all head and neck muscles and letting the eyes stare. At the same time tense hands and arm. Hold for a few seconds and relax slowly out of the position. Repeat once or twice.

Hands

These Hands and Feet exercises help to maintain supple ankles and wrists, toes and fingers.

Fig 1: Stand or sit in a comfortable position and make fists of your hands.

Fig 2: Suddenly snap out the fingers, tensing the muscles as firmly as you can. Repeat several times.

Fig 3: Let hands and wrists go limp and then shake them vigorously.

Fig 2

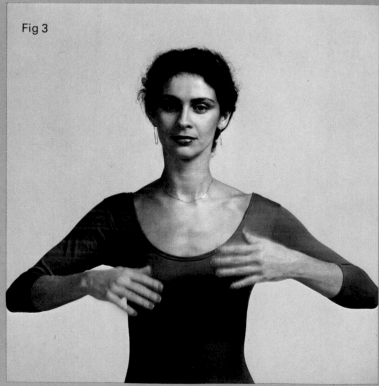

Fig 3

Feet

Fig 1: Sitting on the ground, with legs in front of you, pick up one ankle and draw it up close to the hips. Let the ankle go slack and then shake the leg vigorously so that the foot flops about.

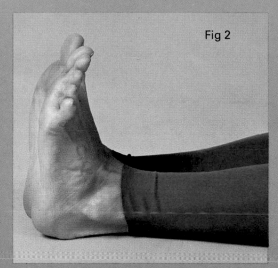

Fig 2: Sitting with the legs stretched in front of you, pull the toes as far towards you as you can.

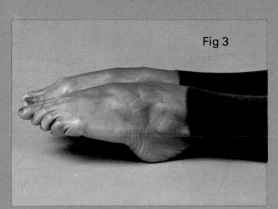

Fig 3: Then push them firmly away, stretching the instep. Repeat several times. Retain awareness of the breath even during these simple exercises.

Head

Flexibility in the neck will save much tension, and eye strain can be reduced with a simple exercise.

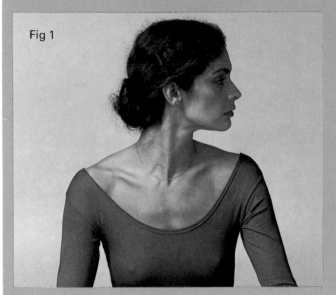

Fig 1

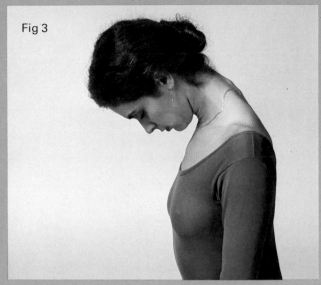

Fig 3

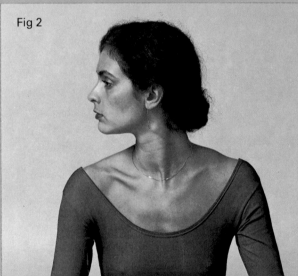

Fig 2

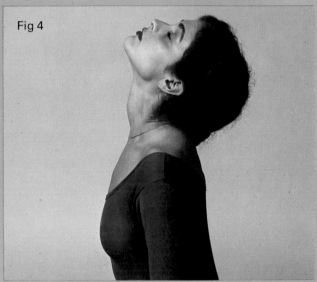

Fig 4

Fig 1: Sitting comfortably, but erect, balance your head on your shoulders and breathe in, looking ahead. Then, breathing out, very slowly turn the head to the left. Do not strain, but maintain the movement with the breath to provide a good stretch. Then come slowly back to the front, breathing in.

Fig 2: Breathing out, turn the head similarly to the right and back again, breathing in. Do all this slowly in coordination with the breath and repeat two or three times.

Fig 3: Breathing out, drop the head so the chin is resting on the chest.

Fig 4: Breathing in, slowly let the head fall back, stretching the front of the neck and the chin. Repeat two or three times.

Eyes

Fig 1

Fig 1: Rub the hands vigorously together to make them warm and increase the electro-magnetic force.

Fig 2

Fig 2: Cup the hands over the eyes and maintain this position for at least 30 seconds, breathing gently. Repeat two or three times. This is particularly effective for tired eyes.

The Pose of Total Relaxation

Lying on a carpet or mat in this position has been an integral part of yoga for many centuries. It is called Sarvasana, which literally means the pose of death or the corpse – in other words, the way a body naturally falls when life has departed, rigor mortis is over and everything in the body is slack. It appears simple, but this can be deceptive for relaxation is something which the majority of people find hard to achieve. It is, however, vital, since it allows the body to normalize, and a whole process, essential to our health, is started from the hypothalamus gland. The aim is to relax the body and still the mind.

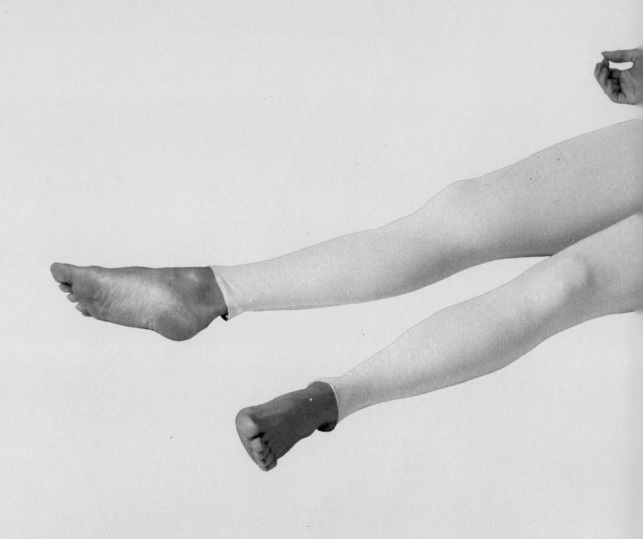

When practicing relaxation, adopt these steps:
(i)   Sit down, with the legs bent and then place the trunk and back of the head on the ground, with the back flat against the ground.
(ii) Slowly straighten the legs, keeping the feet about 18 inches apart and do not allow the back to hollow as the legs straighten.
(iii) Raise the trunk a few inches by supporting it on your elbows, then let the head drop back until it is taking the weight of the trunk. Then slide the trunk down again by letting the head slide back, maintaining its contact with the ground. This will help to bring the shoulders against the ground.
(iv) Let the arms lie out away from your trunk with the palms upwards.
(v)   Make sure the ankles are slack, so that the toes fall outwards.
(vi) Ensure the head is in a straight line with the navel.

When you are sure of your position, *observe* the breath and feel the tummy slowly rising and falling as you breathe. Do not do anything but observe. The state is not one of sleep but heightened awareness; however if you do doze off, do not worry – you probably needed the cat nap. As you continue relaxing the need will pass.

Understanding our Minds

As you progress with performing the yoga postures, carefully linked with correct breathing and mental concentration, you will find your mind becoming a more precise instrument. It is a sobering thought that we often cannot listen to a simple instruction and obey it accurately. This shows that our minds are sometimes functioning in confusion and our decisions are muddled and much of our thought process blurred.

Uncontrolled, the mind is like a naughty child: it persists in doing all the things it is told not to do. If we lose our temper with such a child, we only make matters worse. We have to combine understanding with firmness.

Reaching Peace of Mind

Let us be quite clear that controlling the mind's activities is the most important development we can achieve, for our life, our happiness and our peacefulness depend upon it. Therefore, as you progress in the postures, so other techniques can be applied, gently but persistently. Mastering the approach to the postures first is important so that you can achieve the initial break-through. It must be emphasized that it is not how well you perform the postures that matters, but how you approach them – with clarity and understanding.

Controlling your mind consists of enabling it to dwell on one image, one sound, one word, one thought, without other thoughts providing distraction. At first, this is immensely difficult – gentle persistence is the only way.

Full concentration on the bodily movements of the postures is an immense help in achieving the break-through. Any attempt at stilling your mind must be accompanied by awareness of your breath. The quiet rhythm of the energy flow through the body can help immeasurably in calming you; without it the task is well-nigh impossible.

First Steps in Relaxation

As with Hatha yoga practice (the form of yoga which includes the postures), mind-calming techniques should be practiced in a comfortable room, free from draughts, either on a carpeted floor or on a mat. You should sit in an easy cross-legged position and make sure that the spine is erect, so the back follows its natural slightly concave curve; everything else should be relaxed. If you do not find this comfortable, practice the position but without trying to still the mind, because physical discomfort will always impede mental control. It is quite all right to sit in a straight-backed chair, feet together, toes pointing to the front, spine erect and the rest of the body relaxed. Let one hand rest in the other on your lap.

When you feel you have a correct and comfortable position, close your eyes and become aware of your breath. It is calm, rhythmical and slow because you are quietening yourself. You are establishing yourself as the master of your breath; by so doing, you are mastering your own flow of energy; by mastering your energy you are establishing that you have control of your mind.

As you breathe in, feel the cool touch of the air on your nostrils and, as you breathe out, feel the warm flow of air through them. Be aware that the breathing is slow and that your exhalation is considerably slower than your inhalation. You are controlling the breath. You should practice this quietly and gently several times before you attempt any other technique. As random thoughts come into the mind, gently and persistently push them away. Once this quiet breathing rhythm begins to become natural to you, you can try some further exercises.

Each of these wheels has a *mantra* on the inside of the cover; they are rotated to repeat the prayer.

Like many *mandalas,* this one contains a squared circle, but every detail has spiritual significance.

Candle Gazing

One often-used technique is to take a candle and place it in front of you, three or four feet from you. Then sit as I have described, start to control the breath gently and gaze steadily at the flame of the candle. Keep gazing at the flame: become aware only of the flame, its shape, its movement, its coloring. After you have studied this with a clear gaze for some time, close your eyes and cup your hands over them. See the flame of the candle, bright and clear, in your mind's eye and quietly try to maintain the image. Only when it finally fades, open your eyes. You can repeat the pattern two or three times, so you become more and more adept at it. A *mandala* is a design in which the whole pattern leads you to the center. Gazing steadily at a mandala helps to center your thoughts and to bring you to the required state of single-minded concentration.

More Aids to Concentration

Returning to purely mental images, many people find they can acquire control and peace of mind by the silent repetition of words or sentences. These are called *mantras*. A sense of one-ness, and therefore of peace, can be obtained by sitting quietly and correctly, first of all thinking of the breath and then repeating to oneself the sentence: "I am in life . . . life is in me". The first part can mentally be repeated during the inhalation, the latter part during the exhalation, so the words are intoned rhythmically. Push away any other thoughts and keep coming back to the mantra. Such a thought brings to us the awareness of the universal pattern of life and we relax into this gentle and desirable state.

The act of chanting, either silently or else out loud, is probably as old as language-speaking man himself. The sound of "Om" (which is made up of three distinct parts: Oh-Au-Mm) has for thousands of years been regarded as the basic vibration. It is sometimes also called the primal sound of God. From the sound of Om comes the Christian chant of Amen.

Chanting "Om" can be a tremendous aid to group meditation. Individual meditation can also be enhanced by the repetition of this sound, either chanted out loud or silently. The three parts making up the sound also represent the three basic factors of life: Creation, Preservation and Destruction – out of which again springs Creation.

Techniques of concentration and mind-stilling must always be practiced gently and calmly. While they must be adhered to persistently, there must never be any tension about them. The secret is acceptance. It is a good idea to try to practice these techniques every day at the same time. In this way the mind is quickly conditioned to recognize the time as a period to ease off and the thoughts will thus become more controlled. Success with mind-control will transform your life.

The sacred word "Om" is represented by this *mantra.* The curves portray the physical, mental and supramental states, dominated by the dot of truth or reality.

Understanding our Diet

There is an often-repeated phrase: "You are what you eat". An alternative and better phrase is: "You eat what you are". Many of us eat too much and a great deal of de-vitalized food. We must remember that eating, like everything else, is a natural process. If we have to be too aware of our diet and consciously avoid eating certain foodstuffs, then there is something wrong with us. Your body tells you what food it wants and this intuitive knowledge is quite different from the purely mental reaction built up by social conditioning, advertising and so on. The body craves for natural and fresh foods. All too often we push into the body far too many things which it does not want, which it even tells us will be harmful. We ignore the messages – and we suffer.

Our Bodies' Real Wants

Yoga helps us in our eating habits because as we become more involved with yoga we become happier, more contented people and this automatically alters our attitude to eating. An experiment was carried out with a group of children who were given the opportunity of eating whatever they liked over a period of time. At first they all stuffed themselves with candy and convenience foods – the things they had been conditioned to regard as the most desirable. But after a short while their habits changed and they began to eat other things: quite soon they were eating fruit and raw vegetables in preference to the candy. They had satiated their bodies with the rubbish foods and learned that what their bodies really desired was good, fresh wholesome food. The important fact is that they had learned the lesson naturally and not because people had preached at them.

Yoga helps us to learn the same lesson naturally. As it helps us to obtain greater mental control, to develop rather than to impede the body's energy and to feel more

If you practice yoga and listen to what your body tells you, you will soon find that you turn to more natural foods.

peaceful and fulfilled, we begin to eat more naturally.

Which Foods are Best?

Many arguments are strenuously discussed these days: white bread versus brown bread; refined sugar versus raw sugar; dairy products versus vegetable products. You can read the arguments and the counter arguments until your head spins. There is only one final criterion: if you feel healthy and well and at peace, you will listen to what your body tells you it wants. All the facts and figures and disputes between interested parties pale into insignificance beside this criterion.

Yoga and Vegetarianism

Classically, yoga has largely been practiced by those who follow a vegetarian diet, eating fresh – often raw – vegetables and fruit

If your mind and body are in tune with one another you will want the foods which are good for you, in amounts that leave you slim and healthy.

with cereal and pulses, dairy products and fresh milk. To some degree such an attitude to food is based on culture and climate; in the West these considerations may result in a different diet. The important thing is that diet should be natural and that it should be what we actually want to eat and not what others tell us we want. The trend toward fresh and more natural foodstuffs has accelerated in recent years and is by no means confined to those who follow yoga. It is all part of a new approach to living.

Above all, yoga preaches the middle way: not too little; not too much. Becoming a food faddist in the name of healthy living can be wholly counter-productive.

Practice and Progress

If you have studied this book thus far, you will have a good, working concept of the basic approach to yoga. There are many other more detailed books on the subject. Some may well be extremely helpful, but beware of giving yourself mental indigestion. Some people, when they come to a subject such as yoga, try to embrace everything all at once and make their lives more, rather than less, confused. Dr Rammurti Mishra, a leading exponent of yoga, points out that there is really only one book: the book of our own mind. All knowledge is contained within us and we need only to learn how to search for it. Good books, good speakers, good yoga practitioners, all help us in our search. They do not teach us: they enable us to make discoveries for ourselves. It is for this reason that I have tried in this book to keep to the bare essentials of yoga – for this is precisely what we need. We all need to search for simplicty, rather than complexity. As we develop in our search, we find that more and more things we believed to be complicated are really very simple indeed.

The Right Time to Practice

The practice of yoga, therefore, should be carried through with clear-minded understanding. Take no notice of the old cry, "I haven't got time for it", for yoga is life and that cry merely means we haven't got time to live! So far as your personal practice of the yoga postures is concerned, it is worth while making a real effort to set aside a certain amount of time each day and to carry out the practice at the same hour and in the same place. There is a practical, not a mystical, reason for this. We are all creatures of conditioned reflexes. Much of our daily activity is simply reflex action. We tend, for example, automatically to think of lunch in the middle of the day, not necessarily because we are hungry but because we usually eat then and the brain switches on the necessary messages.

These reflexes can be detrimental to us, if they have been conditioned for the wrong reason. Mass advertising these days tries to impose such reflexes on us to sell commercial products. But reflexes can also be helpful to us, if we understand and use them correctly.

If, therefore, you practice your yoga postures at the same time and in the same place, this will quickly become a mental pattern and the brain will accept it and co-operate. It will become much easier for you to relax correctly through this reflex action. If, however, such regularity is not possible, do not worry. A small advantage has been lost but there is still plenty of scope for advancement.

When practicing either physical or mental techniques, you should seek to avoid draughts. As far as possible it is also important to keep warm, but beware of becoming over-sensitive to heat and cold. If it is a bit chilly, do try to imagine warmth or take reasonable precautions to keep the circulation moving. Don't just feel sorry for yourself. On the other hand, remember that a feeling of chilliness does tense up the muscles, so stretch gently but thoroughly before trying any taxing position.

Yoga in Our Daily Lives

The most important thing is to realize the wholeness of yoga and the fact that it is central to our whole approach to life. With the awareness which yoga brings, you should not fall into the trap of maintaining a bad posture for any length of time without correcting and counterbalancing it. This can affect us throughout the day, whatever we are doing. Once your body has told you how good it feels to be used correctly, you will have the stimulus to work on this. The need to quieten the mind, too, is also vital. Don't let yourself get worked up; don't go on getting more and more wound-up. Remember that

The Mahareshi Maheshi Yogi with some of his followers.

you can always take a minute or two off to calm yourself to help you face the problems squarely.

The more you integrate the natural approach of yoga into your daily life, the quicker your progress will be. Never regard it simply as a physical or mental practice to be tucked away in a daily twenty-minute session. Once you have really absorbed the yoga approach you can set your own target – or be content to set none at all. Most of the limitations that we feel beset us are self-imposed. We are full of feelings of inadequacy and yet we are hardly touching our real capacity.

The Limits of Yoga

Some people allow themselves to be excited at the prospects of paranormal powers – *siddhis*, they are called. This is a snare and a delusion. One of the most celebrated yoga leaders of this century, Swami Sivananda, wrote: "Yoga is not for attaining powers. If a student of yoga is tempted to obtain powers, his further progress is seriously retarded and he has lost his way". So do not get enthusiastic at the prospect of levitation and the other mysteries which are offered by some people.

Even if attainable, such powers are useless in practical terms.

What we all seek is greater peace of mind, a true feeling of fulfilment, good physical health and fitness and a constant feeling of energy and vitality. Correctly understood and practiced, yoga can give you these boons and that in itself is more than sufficient. What a changed world we would live in if we all had such a transformation in our lives.

It is possible, but only you yourself can achieve it – nobody can do it for you. This is perhaps the greatest lesson we have to absorb these days, for we live in a society which seeks to make us more and more dependent. True self-reliance is played down because it is not compatible with an aquisitive society, but that society is itself crumbling, and without self-reliance we can easily find we have nothing.

In health matters we have become accustomed to expect others to put us right. This operates even at the simplest level. For example, from television we learn not proper and sensible eating but the desirability of taking various tablets to relieve the indigestion we have caused wthin us! Once we begin to learn to listen to ourselves at all levels – body, breath and mind – we will find that life takes on a new meaning.

63

Index

Published by Chartwell Books Inc., A Division of Book Sales Inc., 110 Enterprise Avenue, Secaucus, New Jersey 07094. ISBN 0–89009–290–7: L of C No. 79–52933